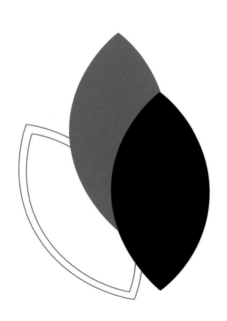

# CALISSON

**FROM LE ROY RENÉ**

# NOUGAT

— Recipes of Provence —

Photography
MARIE-PIERRE MOREL

Text
MARIE-CATHERINE DE LA ROCHE

# FOREWORD

*by* **Olivier Baussan**

# LE ROY RENÉ IS CELEBRATING ITS CENTENARY

Provence is my life.

I grew up near Ganagobie, a tiny village perched on a ridge an hour away from Aix-en-Provence. The tireless working of the land by Benedictine monks has made this place a tranquil haven. The view from the priory encompasses the Durance valley, the Pays de Forcalquier, the Lure mountain and Les Mées plateau, which my father dreamed of replanting with almond trees. As a teenager, I would stride along its footpaths with him. Walking among old tree trunks contorted by the years, survivors of a time when Aix was the almond capital of the world, he would say to me "One day, you'll do it." Like Giono and his "man who planted trees," he wanted to revive the age-old cultivation of this land. He was never able to realize his dream, and I inherited it. Initially, lavender was the central factor, with the creation of L'Occitane en Provence, and I remain closely involved with growers to protect this heritage in our region. When I founded Oliviers & Co, then Première Pression Provence, and later created the Écomusée de l'Olivier (Olive Tree Ecomuseum), I got very involved with the plan to re-establish olive trees that my friend André Pinatel had initiated with Olivier en Provence. In 2014, fate caused my path to cross with that of Le Roy René, and with my father's dream to see almond trees once again flourishing on the Provençal hillsides. This iconic family business, conveyor of the traditions and skills of the *nougatiers* and *calissoniers* of Aix-en-Provence since 1920, has become my own.

An almond-paste smile, recalling childhood Christmases when the sight of a diamond-shaped box of calissons would send us into ecstasies; reminiscences of stories and legends of Cockaigne, that mythical land of pleasure and plenty; little mouthfuls of pure delight, the ultimate treats, the quintessence of Provence … This anniversary book pays homage to the fine work of its *calissonières* and *nougatiers*, whose craftsmanship is passed on from one generation to the next, and to the true character of this glorious terroir, its orchards, its sun-soaked candied fruits and its lavender honey, which have assured the reputation of Le Roy René's calissons and nougats. And, to ensure that the celebrations are even more delicious, we have given free rein to five chefs to lend their touch to these almond- and pistachio-stuffed delicacies and create ten recipes with a twist.

One hundred years is a majestic gift, and it's a gift that, with Laure Pierrisnard, the firm's general manager, we wanted to share with you in this book. From Le Roy René's illustrious past to its flavorful present, we invite you to take a journey to the land of the nougats and calissons of Aix, the Lucullus Rex of a Provence that, based on its history, can be proud of its future.

# CONTENTS

**Previous page:**
A field of lavender with
flowering almond trees on
the Valensole plateau,
Puimoisson, France.

# Once upon a time …
# THE CANDIES OF PROVENCE

# A SWEET
## CENTURY

"WHEN THE GOOD LORD BEGINS TO DOUBT THE WORLD, HE REMEMBERS THAT HE CREATED PROVENCE," WROTE FRÉDÉRIC MISTRAL, NOBEL PRIZE FOR LITERATURE. AND, WHO KNOWS, PERHAPS HE ALSO REMEMBERS THAT PROVENCE CREATED THE CALISSON, THE DIVINE CANDY THAT HAS BEEN LE ROY RENÉ'S PRIDE AND GLORY FOR THE PAST 100 YEARS.

### FROM VENICE
### TO AIX-EN-PROVENCE

In the beginning was the almond, fruit of the Mediterranean Eden. But the tales of the origins of nougat and calisson hail from far and wide. The earliest allusion to calisson is found in a twelfth century manuscript written in medieval Italian Latin, where the word *calissone* is used to describe an almond cake similar to marzipan. This confectionery reappears in *Les Estoires de Venise* (The History of Venice) by Martino da Canale in 1275, while in Crete, people were enjoying *kalitsounia*, made from almond paste and walnuts. In France, legend has it that in 1454, a pastry chef from Aix-en-Provence invented the calisson as we know it today in honor of Jeanne Laval, Roy René's bride-to-be, making this diamond-shaped confectionery a royal delicacy. One thing that is certain is that by the early sixteenth century, the calisson had become the emblem of Aix-en-Provence. In Iardin deys musos provensalos (The Garden of Provençal Muses), which tells of the building of the Château de Cocagne, the poet Claude Brueys wrote: "It was agreed that the house would be built of small cakes, and that the roofs, both large and small, would be covered with tarts and calissons." From then on, almonds were grown in Provence, and Aix became the center of the almond trade. It was the beginning of the spectacular rise to fame of nougat and calisson and of a Provençal passion.

## A FAMILY STORY

In 1920, with the Roaring Twenties stimulating the hunger to live life to the full, Ernest Guillet took over a small confectionery shop in the center of Aix-en-Provence that smelled wonderfully of toasted almonds, candied melon, honey, and pistachio. Here, in their cauldrons, these treasures conceived by the earth and the Provençal sunshine were transformed into small sweet miracles that had the region in raptures. So delicious were they that their fame quickly spread, and Ernest's nougats and calissons soon became the most coveted confectionery in Aix.

In 1947, his son René took over the shop and decided to focus on calissons. On their distinctive diamond-shaped box, he inscribed the words "Calissons du Roy René," which from then on became the name of the "maison."

In 1980, it was the turn of Anne, René's daughter, and Maurice Farine to take over the reins. Maurice was not from Provence, but having traveled around the world as a diplomat, he was ready to settle down. Although Avignon was tempting, he finally decided on Aix: "It's a marvelous thing to wake up every morning under Cézanne's sky!" Here, he fell in love with calissons, which he discovered for the first time in his life: "a smile that lights up the face," he says. When René offered him a partnership in the business, he didn't hesitate for a second. It was obvious to him that Le Roy René's calissons needed to be introduced to the whole of France, that they needed to be marketed much more widely and become ambassadors for Provence. With the passion of a conquistador, he embraced the calisson cause, determined to share this Provençal treasure with the world. One passion led to another: he and Anne fell in love and got married. The future of Le Roy René calissons was secured with a third generation. The firm was growing and modernizing. But it retained its family spirit and—despite the appearance of a packaging robot—its spirit of craftsmanship, which, as René Guillet used to say, is "the true art and the only good way to make the best calissons in the world." In 2012, Le Roy René became an "Entreprise du Patrimoine Vivant" (a French certification label awarded to companies in recognition of their excellent craftsmanship).

The first Calissons du Roy René shop, at 7 rue Papassaudi, Aix-en-Provence.

**Opposite:**
Botanical illustration of the almond tree (*Amygdalus communis L.*) from the *Atlas des plantes de France utiles, nuisibles et ornementales* (volume 2) by Amédée Masclef, 19th century.

1

B

2

3

A

*Pl. 94.*

*Amandier commun. Amygdalus communis L.*

**Opposite:**
Confectionery packaging
workshop, Aix-en-Provence,
c. 1930.
**Above, top:** Candy and
fruit-paste workshop
(using the "mogul" process),
early 20th century.

**Above:** Interior of
a candied-fruit confectionery,
early 20th century.

The Musée du Calisson tells the **story of the almond trees**, candied fruits, calissons, and **nougats of Provence**. A sheller, the original mill, objects, and photographs retrace the **life of the calisson** and nougat makers at the time when Ernest Guillet, in the **1920s**, then René, in the **1950s**, owned the confectionery shop.

Chantal, calissonière
at Le Roy René for
41 productive years.

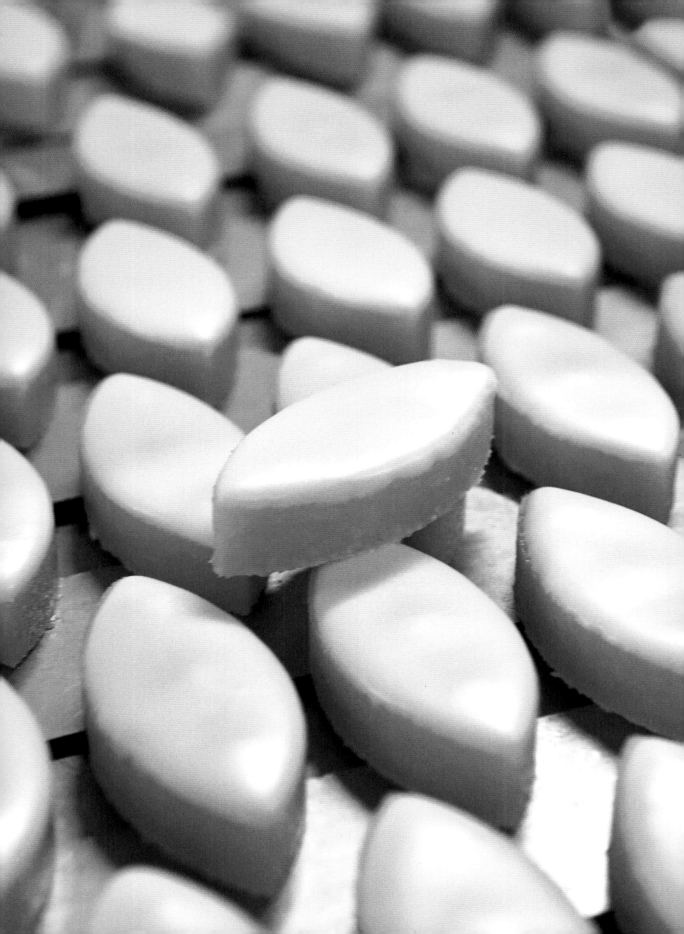

## A PROVIDENTIAL MAN FOR PROVENCE

In three generations, the small shop has become the largest manufacturer of Calissons d'Aix. In 2014, Anne and Maurice began looking for a successor who would be a custodian of Le Roy René's expertise. Olivier Baussan, the founder of L'Occitane en Provence, already had a lot on his plate, but he immediately fell in love with this Provençal beauty and became the new "master of the house." As a lifelong ecologist—he has spent his life fighting to restore the fragrance of its lavender and the prestige of its olive groves to Haute-Provence—Baussan found a new project to devote himself to. With calissons and nougats, he saw the opportunity to revitalize the cultivation of almond and pistachio trees which had once shaped the Provençal landscape. "At the dawn of the First World War, we were the world's leading almond producers. Today, less than 1% come from France! It is said that there were once 800,000 almond trees on the Valensole plateau. Pistachio trees have had the same fate. Today, their country has become America," he laments. He mustered former associates—the vanguard of the regeneration of olive trees—including André Pinatel, who for many years chaired the Alpes de Haute-Provence Chamber of Agriculture, set up a relaunch plan and created the Syndicat des Producteurs d'Amande de Provence. The goal: to plant 1000 hectares (2471 acres) of almond trees in five years. Four hundred hectares (just under 1000 acres) have already been established. The producers embarking on this adventure know that the fruit of their labors will be used to make Aix calissons and nougats. Le Roy René alone uses 200 tons of almonds every year. The first pistachio trees have also made a comeback. In a virtuous circle of repatriated cultivation, Provence is revitalizing the heart of its terroir, and calissons and nougats are gradually reclaiming local distribution channels.

Montagne Sainte-Victoire
(part of the south face),
Coteaux d'Aix vines
and lavender.

## THE DREAM FACTORY

Maurice Farine had a dream: "to build a wonderful factory." A factory where people could see the confectioners at work, immerse themselves in the fascinating and magical world of calissons and nougats. He created the setting for this dream with Marseille architect Christophe Gullizy: a contemporary, environmentally friendly building made of 1000 blocks of Castillon stone—the same age-old, calisson-colored stone used in the Pont du Gard. This was the "wonderful factory" that Olivier Baussan discovered on his arrival. He has joined his own dream to Maurice's. On its roof, 1200 solar panels draw energy from the Provençal sunshine. With its waste sorting, treatment and recycling of wastewater, and heat pumps, Le Roy René has been certified as a "Bâtiment Durable Méditerranéen" (sustainable Mediterranean building). The factory also has its own almond grove: 300 almond trees have been planted on the hillside overlooking it. A dozen hives are regularly brought down from the mountain and take a vacation here for pollination. And, in the small Eden of a Bastide garden, such as traditional Provençal houses used to possess, La Calissonne roses, Golden Achillea, and medicinal and aromatic plants flourish in an ancestral orchard. Nineteen varieties are the custodians of the biodiversity of French almond trees.

A blossoming almond orchard with beehives for pollination (Lauranne and Ferragnès, Charleval).

## CALISSONS AND NOUGATS ENTER THE MUSEUM

During the Trojan War, a ship bringing home Demophon, son of Theseus and Phaedrus, ran aground in the Aegean Sea. There, Demophon fell in love with Phyllis, Princess of Thrace. He had to go home but promised to return. Time passed and Phyllis, devoured by grief, took her own life. Taking pity on the princess's lifeless body, the goddess Hera turned it into a bare tree. When he returned, Demophon, rushing to the tree, embraced it with all his strength. The tree became covered with flowers, then leaves, and became an almond tree—a symbol of their fragile and virginal love. This legend, inscribed beneath a huge painting of a flowering almond tree, welcomes visitors to the museum. Created on the first floor of the factory on the initiative of Olivier Baussan, this museum invites visitors to discover the history of Provence's almond trees, candied fruits, calissons, and nougats. A guide—occasionally Maurice Farine, who has become a sort of oral historian of the firm—tells the tale of the origins of these candies of a king and princess and reveals the secret of their ingredients and their manufacture. A sheller, the original mill, objects, and photographs retrace the life of the calisson and nougat makers at the time when Ernest Guillet, in the 1920s, and René, in the 1950s, owned the confectionery shop, while visitors can look down onto the workings of the modern factory through huge windows. In the center, like an insatiable ogre, a "millipede" robot grabs five calissons per second. But while new technologies have burst onto the scene and some machines are now semi-automatic, their operation remains modeled on ancestral handicrafts that have been passed down from generation to generation. The same processes continue to be used to transform raw almonds into calissons and nougats.

# A PROVENÇAL
## SAGA

ROYAL EPICS, CHRISTMAS TALES, MIRACULOUS LEGENDS,
BOXES OF TRICKS: NOUGATS AND CALISSONS FEATURE IN
A WEALTH OF STORIES. ANECDOTES AND EPICS, FULL OF
FLAVORS, MIX MAGIC INTO THESE TASTY TREATS. THEY ARE
THE DELICIOUS STORY OF PROVENCE.

### FOR A QUEEN'S SMILE

Legend has it that calissons were born of a desire to put a smile on the lips of Jeanne de Laval. In 1445, good King René, Count of Provence, Duke of Anjou, King of Naples, Sicily and Jerusalem, was widowed. He decided to remarry, and chose for his bride the beautiful Jeanne, twenty-four years his junior, who was "very virtuous and wise," to the point that she was reputed to be somewhat austere. On the eve of the wedding, King René asked his pastry chef to create a treat that would make his young bride smile. The chef concocted a confectionery made from almonds and candied melons, covered with royal icing. René offered it to Jeanne. As soon as she tasted it, her face lit up. The court, surprised and curious, asked: "What do you call these candies that are making the queen smile?" To which the king is said to have replied "*Di calin soun*"—they're *câlins*, cuddles! According to legend, the next day, the pastry chef, prompted by the success of his creation, decided to rework his *calisson*, which he had made in a diamond shape, curving the edges to give them the contours of the queen's smile. But as attractive as this legend is, it was not until the introduction of almonds to Provence in the sixteenth century and the growth of its cultivation locally, that Aix became established as the city of "*câlins*."

Traditional Provençal costumes at the Blessing of Calissons, Aix-en-Provence, September 1, 2019.

## A TASTE OF THE SACRED

Of course, it is terribly tempting to believe that calissons draw their etymology from *câlins*—cuddles. But according to the scholars, it's more likely that "*calissoum*" was formed from the word *calice* (chalice) and the Provençal diminutive suffix *-oun*. In other words, the word probably refers to a "little chalice," which is all the more likely as its base is a wafer.

This etymology harks back to another legend. When, in 1630, Aix-en-Provence was ravaged by the plague, the Parliament of Provence and the terrified magistrates fled the city. Soon, there remained only the provost of the Mimata chapter, the consul Borilli and the assessor Martelly. On January 20, the latter, leading public figures and the people, went to church to implore the protection of the Vierge de la Seds (Our Lady of the Seds), the patron saint of the city. In order to obtain his request, he made a vow to have a thanksgiving mass celebrated every year on his behalf. From then on, every first Sunday in September, the bells of the city would ring out to call the people of Aix to honor "*le Vœu de Martelly*"—Martelly's vow. Calissons, blessed by the archbishop, would be distributed to the faithful, while singing

"*Venes touti i calissoun*"—"come to the chalice", which mischievous locals soon translated as: "*Venez tous au calisson*"—"Come to the calisson"! This tradition lasted until the Revolution, and since 1995, has been revived by the people of Aix. Laure Pierrisnard, who Olivier Baussan appointed general manager of Le Roy René, and who is also a native of Provence, had the honor of carrying, amid much pomp, Our Lady of the Calissons during the last possession. She relates:

"At 10 o'clock in the morning, the mass to renew Martelly's vow is held at the Saint-Sauveur Cathedral. Then the procession heads to the Cours Mirabeau, where its arrival is greeted with folk music and dancing. The procession resumes its route to the forecourt of the Church of St. John of Malta. There, baskets of calissons, carried around the neck by young women dressed in traditional costume, are blessed. Father Daniel delivers an address, in the caricatural spirit of the priest of Cucugnan in Alphonse Daudet's *Letters from My Windmill*, and finally the calissons are distributed. It all ends in singing and dancing. It's a wonderful Provençal celebration in honor of the almonds and calissons of Aix."

## FOR THE LOVE OF A PRINCESS

Nougat, too, has its mythology. It is said that an apprentice confectioner, desperately in love with a princess, one day dedicated a recipe of his own invention to her. Inspired by his passion for the beautiful woman, he poured into a copper cauldron, honey for her golden hair, almonds for the shape of her eyes, and sugar for her sweetness. From the alchemy of these ingredients emerged nougat. It's a beautiful fairy tale, steeped in love, but the true origins of nougat remain a mystery. Indeed, a certain Monsieur de Nougarède du Hasset took such an avid interest in the matter that he spent fifty-five years of his life writing an 8721-page manuscript, without managing to solve the enigma. One thing is certain, however, and that is that from the tenth century, traces of this displaced delicacy have been found, under different names, from Baghdad to Aleppo, from Bukhara to Cairo, from Phoenicia to Greece, and from Andalusia to Catalonia, where it's known as *torron*.

Blessing of Calissons: Our Lady of the Calissons leaves the Église Saint-Jean de Malte on September 1, 2019, carried by Laure Pierrisnard, President of the Union des fabricants de calisson d'Aix (French union of calisson makers), and Serge Billet, Provost of the Compagnons des calissons (professional association of master calisson makers).

The **procession** heads to the Cours Mirabeau, where its arrival is greeted with **folk music** and dancing. It then resumes its route to the forecourt of the Church of St. John of Malta. There, **baskets of calissons**, carried around the neck by young women dressed in **traditional costume**, are blessed.

Baskets of calissons blessed by Monseigneur Christophe Dufour, the Archbishop of Aix-en-Provence and Arles, September 1, 2019.

## FROM NOSTRADAMUS TO THE DUKES' PLEASURE

In France, in 1555, the famous astrologer and apothecary Nostradamus—who lived all his life in Provence—provided a recipe in his *Treaty of Jams* for white nougat with almonds called "*pignolat*," which he presented as originating in Italy. The word also appears in 1595 in a pharmaceutical book and in 1607 in a nutrition book, *Le Thresor de santé* (The Health Treasury). There is no doubt that people had been biting into dark nougat in Provence for a long time before then, however. Some say that this delicacy arrived with the Phoenicians, who founded Marseille in the sixth century BC and who allegedly brought with them from the East a delicacy made from nuts and honey: *nux gatum*. That aside, it is a fact that by the end of the seventeenth century, confectioners in Provence were becoming famous for their nougat. Thanks to the work of soil scientist Olivier de Serres, it became possible to cultivate almond trees in the South of France. He planted them in particular in the region around Montélimar. Nougat began to be produced there in the form we know today and quickly became hugely popular with candy lovers. It was a success story that quickly spread throughout France. In January 1701, Louis, Duke of Burgundy and future father of Louis XV, and Charles of Valois, Duke of Berry, Louis XIV's grandson, were passing through Montélimar. Claude Souchon, First Consul of the city, offered them a *quintal* (equivalent to 42kg/93lb) of nougat to accompany them on their journey. This was the beginning of nougat's renown.

**Previous pages and opposite:**
Traditional costumes worn during the Blessing of Calissons, Église Saint-Jean de Malte, September 1, 2019.

**Nougat**, too, has its mythology. It is said that an apprentice confectioner, desperately in love with **a princess**, one day dedicated a recipe of his own **invention** to her. Inspired by his passion for the beautiful woman, he poured into a copper cauldron, **honey** for her golden hair, **almonds** for the shape of her eyes, and **sugar** for her sweetness.

## A CHRISTMAS STORY

It is customary in Provence to serve thirteen desserts at Christmas dinner. The tradition relates to the Lord's Supper, the last meal Jesus ate with his twelve apostles. The desserts are to be served at the same time, on a table covered with three white tablecloths and decorated with three candles, which symbolize the Trinity: God the Father, Jesus the Son, and the Holy Spirit. One of the most important of these desserts is gibassier, a kind of galette made with olive oil and scented with anise or orange blossom. Then come the four *mendiants* (beggars): raisins, dried figs, walnuts, and almonds. And confectionery, which varies from family to family. But, while there may be arguments about what should be included, there's no debating that nougat—both dark and white—and calissons are musts. "My grandmother used to make the dark nougat herself, but she would go to Le Roy René to buy a box of calissons," recalls Laure Pierrisnard. "I would help her arrange all these treasures on plates, very excited at the prospect of eating them and of opening the presents that I would be getting!"

Today, the peak season for calissons remains Christmas. And not only in Provence. Having conquered the whole of France, these little golden treats and their diamond-shaped boxes have become Santa Claus's messengers and, since delighting Queen Jeanne, their almond-paste smiles have brightened the childhood memories of generations.

Pistachios also have their Christmas story. Among the *santons* of Provence (small hand-painted terracotta nativity scene figurines), you will find *le pistachier*—the pistachio grower—a "womanizer." And for good reason: it takes only one male pistachio tree to fertilize nine or ten female ones. This nativity character—and a nickname that French "skirt chasers" regularly get saddled with—attests, in his own way, to the fact that there was a time when the Provençal countryside was covered with pistachio groves.

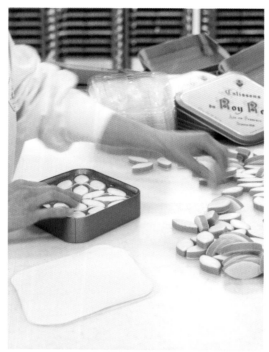

# THE ALMOND, PROVENCE'S GOLD

While the Greeks made the almond tree the tree of eternal love, there is another myth that claims its fruit could cause a virgin to conceive. Young girls were therefore strongly discouraged from falling asleep under its branches while dreaming of their loves! But if the almond is the cause of any guilty desire, it is that of indulgence. For, since ancient times, this gift of the gods has been at the heart of myriad candies. Toasted, slivered, ground, or blanched, in paste, cream, or milk form, the almond is the fruit of all desires. And so, from Iran to Provence and throughout the Mediterranean, the cultivation of *Prunus dulcis*—to give it its pretty botanical name—evolved. Over the centuries and until the First World War, Aix became and remained the world capital of "white-gold" confectioners. Almond picking was at that time done by hand: hemp cloths—*bourras*—were strewn under the branches, which were then struck with a stick to release their fruit. The *bourra* was tied, then loaded on a cart to be brought home. The whole family would gather for the shelling, removing the green part surrounding the seed. Should a shell release a double almond, there was a game that would involve sharing it with one's neighbor. The next day, the first of the pair to greet the other with the words "Bonjour Philippine" would be entitled either to a small gift or to the right to impose a forfeit—either of which could be a kiss! Hence the name "philippine" almond for a double almond, which derives from the German "beloved." Once the shelling was finished, the almonds were left to dry in the sun. Then they would be sifted and calibrated. The tricky and long crushing operation could then begin. It lasted from All Saints' Day to St. Joseph's feast day—in other words, from early November until mid-March—in a cold room, warmed by the shells that would be burned. This work was done by women, often using a stone. Then came the blanching process to remove the thin brown skin, after which the almond is ivory colored. Until 1220, this work provided the pattern of life in the countryside. But when the men departed for the war in 1914, the almond groves were left with no one to tend them, and the big freeze of 1956 finished them off. Today, however, the big comeback of these "virginal" trees is underway—to the benefit of Le Roy René's nougats and calissons.

**Opposite:** Sacks of shelled almonds, Le Roy René factory.

**Above:** Calibration of the raw Provençal almonds, Famille Jaubert, Valensole.

**Right:** Blanching the almonds, Le Roy René factory.

For, since ancient times, this **gift of the gods** has been at the heart of myriad **candies**. Toasted, slivered, ground, or blanched, in paste, cream, or milk form, the almond is the fruit **of all desires**.

# CALISSON:
# 13.3 grams of pleasure

A SUBTLE BLEND OF FINELY GROUND SWEET ALMONDS, CANDIED MELON, AND ORANGE PEEL, SET ON A THIN WAFER BASE AND COVERED WITH ROYAL ICING, THE RECIPE FOR CALISSON D'AIX HAS REMAINED UNCHANGED SINCE ITS CREATION FOR A QUEEN'S PLEASURE. A TRIBUTE TO THESE SOFTEST OF DIAMONDS.

## A MAGIC FORMULA AND THE SECRET OF ITS PRODUCTION

The art and science of creating this delicious royal confectionery have spanned the centuries. The same magic formula has remained sacrosanct since 1454: mix one part of almonds with one part of candied fruit, usually melon, add one part of hot sugar syrup, and you will obtain a lovely calisson paste. But each master confectioner adds their own personal touch, sometimes a jealously guarded secret—some orange peel here, an ounce of candied apricot or lemon there—and their "angels' share." At Le Roy René, it is a drop of bitter almond essential oil that adds the finishing touch to this little gourmet masterpiece.

It may be a little gem, but it lays claim to a great tradition of ancestral expertise. The almonds are already shelled when they arrive at the factory. Here, they are blanched, immersed in a tub of boiling water. Now supple and soft, they join the smooth candied fruits—Cavaillon melon and orange peel—to be rolled between powerful cylinders, transforming them into a long ribbon of paste. Before this concoction can become calisson paste, however, it must be kneaded with a hot sugar syrup. It is at this point that the bitter almond essential oil adds its note, filling the factory with its fragrance. Then comes the waiting time: it takes three days for all the flavors to fully permeate the golden paste. This accomplished, it can finally be formed into calissons.

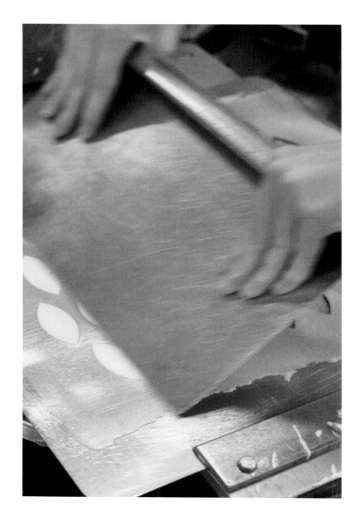

Shaping the Calisson
d'Aix: applying and
smoothing the royal
icing, Le Roy René
factory.

Harvesting melons,
Céreste, Alpes-de-Haute-
Provence, July 2019.

**Opposite and above:** Candying melons and citrus fruits at Apt.

## THE FAMED HANDIWORK OF THE *CALISSONIÈRES*

They always work as a pair. Inseparable, these *calissonière* duos give the factory its reason for being with their "pas de deux." Alexandra and Laure have formed one of these exceptional partnerships. Facing each other on either side of the press, their actions alternate and harmonize with each other with the precision of a choreography, where nothing interrupts the sequence of movements. Alexandra places the wafer under the calisson mold, then releases the paste that will fill the little cups. She levels off the contents and spreads a thin layer of royal icing, made from icing sugar and egg white, on top. Twenty-eight seconds and the tray flips. Laure blocks the latter and activates the pistons that will pierce the wafer and extract the calissons from their molds. Using two "combs," she carefully places the calissons on a baking sheet, which is then put in the oven for 10 minutes to allow the mat and immaculate royal icing to attain a state of perfection. Meanwhile, the dance of the *calissonières*' hands continues, their perfectly synchronized movements giving birth to new calissons.

Making the calisson paste: grinding, cutting, and shaping.

## HOW AIX WON THE CALISSON WAR

This work of the *calissoniers* and *calissonières* nearly fell victim to the affront of globalization. In late 2016, 9,500 kilometers from the home of Le Roy René, in the province of Zhejiang, a Chinese industrialist registered the "Calisson d'Aix" trademark. Olivier Baussan and Laure Pierrisnard, the President of the Union des fabricants de calisson d'Aix (French union of calisson makers), still reminisce about it: the status of calisson was protected in France, but not worldwide! The calisson d'Aix was under threat and there was an urgent need to take action. This offensive could adulterate forever this Provençal gem, whose perfection relies on a triangle of local beatitudes—Mediterranean almonds, Cavaillon melon, candied fruit from Apt—as well as on ancestral knowledge and expertise. There was an uproar. The French union of calisson makers met at Le Roy René's premises. A counter-attack was launched. Pitting David against Goliath, the region of Aix against China, the battle was unequal and fierce, and many thought it would be lost, but for well-made calissons, nothing is impossible. The Chinese Trademark Office eventually surrendered, recognizing the precedence of the French "Calisson d'Aix" trademark. The name-theft attempt had failed. Still, it was a wake-up call to those who had orchestrated this victory for Aix to take more care in the future. Steps were taken to obtain a Protected Geographical Indication (PGI). Never again would the king of calissons be at the mercy of poor workmanship. To be proclaimed "d'Aix," calissons now have to be manufactured in their region of origin, to be made from Mediterranean almonds—so, predominant American ones (California provides nearly 80 percent of the world's almonds) will find no place here—and to contain no less than 12% of candied melon.

Who knows, perhaps one day, Le Roy René will get its own back and open a store in China! Twenty-five countries already have theirs—small Aix enclaves around the world. Half of all calissons sold worldwide are made by Le Roy René.

Le Roy René's marvelous factory and its Calisson Museum —both listed as "Bâtiment Durable Méditerranéen" (sustainable Mediterranean buildings)—can be found on the famous Nationale 7 (the major highway linking Paris to the South of France), in the heart of Provence.

## VARIATIONS IN MINOR AND MAJOR KEYS

To give credit where it is due, the authentic calisson d'Aix remains the mainstay of the company's tradition. But that does not prevent it from varying the pleasures to be had from this candy. In a mini format, it becomes a moreish morsel to enjoy with a cup of coffee or tea. Adorned in an array of colors—it is said that the joyful palette was inspired by Aix's carnival and Harlequin's costume—it takes on new flavors: verbena and citrus, Soliès fig, Burgundy blackcurrant, Corsican clementine. Once a fortnight, Christian Di Falco submits new calissons for tasting: "Some creations are developed in a month; others require a year of testing before the recipe is perfect," he says. Concocted with Michelin-starred chef Pierre Reboul, without any artificial coloring or flavors, this new generation of calissons makes use of seasonal produce and also contains less sugar. "Fruit pulp replaces some of the syrup, and spices are blended with the almonds," says the chef, who, originally from Gap, now heads up one of the best restaurants in Aix. Expanding his realm of pleasure, he has worked for Le Roy René on the creation of calissons that are larger and contain more almonds and fruit and less sugar. Tasty little desserts, fit for a king's tea or a princess's supper, the 35 grams of these deliciously moist calissons *pâtissiers*, in which sugar is reduced to an appropriate level, can be enjoyed at any opportunity without ever feeling over-indulged. The illustrations of these new calissons were created by Olivier Baussan's wife, Bernadette.

Le Roy René has another specialty, which makes desserts even more delicious. Any calisson that presents any sort of defect, drip, or crack is immediately transformed into "calisson cream." "Initially, it was a way to avoid waste and be more environmentally friendly," says Laure Pierrisnard. But this wonderful cream soon found fans. It is delicious as a base for tarts, panna cotta, crème brûlée, and ice cream—and for your imagination to get to work on other culinary creations.

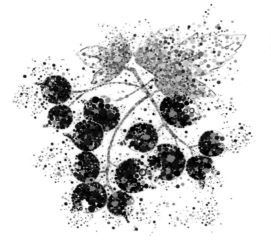

**Opposite:** The calissons *pâtissiers*—tasty little desserts and treats fit for a king—weigh less than 35 grams each. With blackcurrant or fig, they are deliciously soft.

# MAJESTIC
## NOUGAT

A DREAM OF HONEY AND ALMONDS, AN ORIENTAL DELIGHT AND AN OCCITAN DELICACY, CRUNCHY OR SOFT, SQUARE OR RECTANGULAR, WHITE OR BROWN, NOUGAT IS THE YIN AND YANG OF PROVENÇAL CONFECTIONERY. LE ROY RENÉ'S FIRST LOVE, IT REMAINS AT THE HEART OF THE BUSINESS'S CENTURY-OLD *SAVOIR-FAIRE*. A MAJESTIC PORTRAIT OF THAT MOST INTOXICATING OF SINS: GLUTTONY.

### BLACK AND WHITE MAGIC

Dark nougat—*nougat noir* (black nougat) in French—contains only almonds and honey from Provence. It is the latter, brought to a boil—a delicate operation!—that gives it its color. Toasted almonds are then added. As soon as they begin to "sing"—crack—they are removed from the heat. All that remains then is to pour this mixture between two sheets of edible wafer paper and keep a close eye on it as it sets. A very simple recipe for a very sublime dessert, this nougat is the one that was made at home to be proudly displayed as one of the thirteen Christmas desserts, a tradition that continues in some Provençal families.

Making white nougat is the business of a confectioner. In addition to honey and almonds, it contains beaten egg whites, which give it its soft texture. The almonds are toasted before being incorporated into the mixture, which sometimes also contains pistachios. While white nougat is the counterpart of dark nougat in the thirteen Provençal desserts, it is also a gourmet gift that is offered throughout the year. During the latter half of the nineteenth century, a small revolution took place in its manufacture with the appearance of glucose—liquid sugar that does not crystallize. Mixed with ordinary sugar, it yields a soft nougat that keeps better. It is this nougat, in the same form that we know it today, that made Le Roy René's first small workshop famous and that continues to be central to the activity of its new factories. To the nirvana of the original nougats has been added the mastery of fancy nougats. Organic lemon and orange peel, pistachios, blackcurrant and raspberry, salted butter caramel—and even calisson: delicious new flavors have added fresh surprises to this sweet treat.

## DARK NOUGAT

**Edible wafer paper**
**2 ¼ lb. (1 kg) Provençal flower honey**
**2 ¼ lb. (1 kg) whole almonds**

Line the bottom of a wooden frame with a sheet of edible wafer paper. In a copper bowl, cook the honey over a low heat, stirring continuously with a wooden spoon. Bring to a boil, then add the almonds. When the honey turns brown and the almonds are beginning to crackle, remove from the heat and stir for a few more minutes. Pour the honey into the prepared frame. Cover with another sheet of wafer paper, place a board on top and weight it down. Leave the nougat to cool completely before cutting it into pieces.

*Recipe from* La Cuisinière provençale *(1897) by Jean-Baptiste Reboul*

## THE *NOUGATIER*,
## CRAFTSMAN OF PERFECTION

The job of a *nougatier* requires skill. Patrice Alibert, a *pâtissier-chocolatier* by training, has been at Le Roy René for nine years. He inherited his *savoir-faire* from his predecessor. Because more than simply a job, being a *nougatier* is about practicing an art that can be acquired only by being passed on from one person to another. Humidity and the ingredients used will affect the cooking time and the speed at which the *nougatier* must work. Nougat is not made in the same way in autumn as it is in spring and the process can even vary from one day to the next. As Patrice explains with passion: "You have to bring the honey to melting point in the cooking pot until it makes a little ball between your fingers. In the bain-marie, whip up the egg whites, with a little honey, until fluffy. At the same time, you have to prepare the syrup, from water, sugar and glucose, which also needs to be at the perfect temperature. It is incorporating all these elements at exactly the right moment that will give the nougat its soft and airy texture."

When this mixture has turned bright white, and the *nougatier* senses that it is ready, it is time to add the toasted almonds, bright green pistachios, dried fruits, or whatever, depending on the recipe, and, as a final touch, a little confectioners' sugar. Once it has been spread out by rollers, in large molds lined with sheets of edible wafer paper, the nougat needs to be left to set for 24 hours before being cut into rectangles or voluptuous little squares. All that remains now is to enjoy it. "And you don't need a recipe for that!"

To the nirvana of the original nougats has been added the mastery of fancy nougats. Organic lemon and orange peel, pistachios, blackcurrant and raspberry, salted butter—and even calisson: **delicious new flavors** have added **fresh surprises** to this **sweet treat**.

La Nougaterie du Roy René's packaging has taken on a new lease of life with the new nougat collection.

## OLIVIER BAUSSAN'S DREAM

Guardian of unique recipes and expertise, driven by the passion of its *nougatiers* and *calissonières*, who are proud to continue its hundred-year heritage, Le Roy René has managed to retain its artisanal soul. Even better, Olivier Baussan's dream is today on the way to becoming a reality. Almond and pistachio trees are making their comeback in Provence. A blessing for calissons and nougat, the confectionery and pride of both Aix-en-Provence and Le Roy René.

# Majestic
# PROVENÇAL
# TREATS

Five chefs have been busy cooking: Laila Aouba, head chef at Yard, a gastro-pub and wine bar; Christophe Felder, cake maestro, founder of a patisserie school in Strasbourg and author of many prize-winning books, who has a patisserie in Mutzig; Georgiana Viou, recipient of numerous culinary awards and soon-to-be chef at Tindjan in Marseille; Patrice Gelbart, creator of eco-friendly dishes at Youpi, the successful restaurant at the Théâtre de Gennevilliers; and Stéphane Jégo, the chef with a cause at Chez l'Ami Jean in Paris. All nuts about nougat and calissons, they have given them a tender and crispy interpretation, with their own fine-food flair, drawing inspiration from a childhood where almonds, flavored with melon or coated in honey, reigned supreme.

**LAILA AOUBA**   *Chef, Yard, Paris*

# PARIS-AIX

**Serves 4**
**Prep: 1 hour**
**Cook: 45 minutes**

**For the choux pastry:**

⅓ cup (80 ml) water
⅓ cup (80 ml) milk
⅓ cup (2 ¾ oz./80 g) butter
¾ teaspoon superfine
(caster) sugar
⅓ teaspoon fine salt
⅔ cup (2 3/4 oz./80 g)
all-purpose (plain) flour
3 whole eggs + 1 yolk,
for glazing
Chopped almonds and
confectioners' (icing) sugar,
for decorating

**For the calisson mousseline
cream:**

2 cups (500 ml) milk
3 tablespoons calisson cream
6 egg yolks
Scant 1 tablespoon superfine
(caster) sugar
⅓ cup (1 ½ oz./40 g)
all-purpose (plain) flour
Scant 1 cup (200 ml)
whipping cream

Make the choux pastry. In a saucepan, bring the water, milk, and butter to a boil with the sugar and salt. Add the flour all at once, remove from the heat, and stir quickly with a spatula until the dough comes away from the sides of the pan. Transfer the dough to the bowl of a mixer fitted with a flat beater and emulsify by adding the eggs one at a time. When the dough is smooth, place it carefully into a pastry (piping) bag fitted with a ½ inch (1 cm) plain tip (nozzle).
Preheat the oven to 360°F (180°C). With a pencil, draw an 8 inch (20 cm) diameter circle on a sheet of baking paper with the aid of a baking circle. Pipe the dough on the line to make a first ring, make a second one inside it, touching the first, then pipe a third one over the top of the first two. Using a pastry brush, brush the dough with the beaten egg yolk and sprinkle with the chopped almonds. Bake in the oven for 40–45 minutes. When the choux pastry has puffed up, open the oven door slightly and leave to cool in the oven.

Make the calisson mousseline cream. In a saucepan, heat the milk with the calisson cream, stirring gently until it has melted. Remove the pan from the heat and leave to come to room temperature. In a bowl, whisk the egg yolks with the sugar until they turn white. Stir in the flour, then add the cooled milk in three lots. Pour the mixture back into the saucepan and heat to 185°F (85°C) so that the cream thickens. Stir well with a spatula to prevent it sticking. Leave to cool completely.
Whisk the whipping cream until it is firm, then stir it into the cooled calisson cream using a spatula. Place the mousseline cream in a pastry (piping) bag fitted with a fluted tip (nozzle) and refrigerate.

To assemble, cut the choux ring in half widthwise and pipe the mousseline cream inside. Cover with the other half, press down lightly with a cooling rack to ensure it is straight, and sprinkle with confectioners' (icing) sugar.

**LAILA AOUBA**    *Chef, Yard, Paris*

# PROVENÇAL-STYLE
# PANNA COTTA

**Serves 4**
**Prep: 20 minutes**
**Cook: 40 minutes**
**Rest: 6 hours**

2 cups (500 ml) whipping
cream
2 tablespoons + 1 teaspoon
calisson cream
3 egg whites
A few strips of candied
orange and/or lemon peel

In a saucepan, heat half of the whipping cream with the calisson cream, stirring constantly. Remove the pan from the heat, leave to cool, then stir in the remaining whipping cream.
Strain the egg whites through a fine sieve, then gradually add them to the cooled cream, while whisking.

Divide the cream among individual containers and add the candied peel. Cover each container with foil and cook in a steam oven or steamer for 35 minutes. Alternatively, cook them in a bain-marie at 325°F (160°C) for 30 minutes.

Leave the panna cotta to cool, then refrigerate for at least 6 hours before serving.

**CHRISTOPHE FELDER**   *Pastry Chef, Strasbourg*

# BOSTOCK
## CALISSON

**Serves 6**
**Prep: 30 minutes**
**Cook: 20 minutes**

10 ½ oz. (300 g) brioche
½ jar of calisson cream
50 almonds, chopped with a
knife and chopped dark nougat
¼ cup unsifted (1 oz./30 g)
confectioners' (icing) sugar

**For the bostock syrup:**
Scant 1 cup (200 ml) water
⅓ cup (2 ½ oz./70 g) superfine
(caster) sugar
½ cup (1 ¾ oz./50 g) slivered
(flaked) almonds
¼ cup unsifted (1 oz./30 g)
confectioners' (icing) sugar
Grated zest of ½ orange
Grated zest of ½ lemon
1 tablespoon of orange
flower water

Make the syrup. In a saucepan, boil the water and sugar until syrupy. Pour this syrup over the slivered (flaked) almonds and confectioners' (icing) sugar in the bowl of a food processor, and mix everything finely. Pour the mixture into a saucepan, add the grated orange and lemon zest, and bring to a boil. Remove from the heat and leave to cool completely, then stir in the orange flower water.

Preheat the oven to 400°C (200°C). Cut the brioche into 1 inch (3 cm) thick slices, then into regular squares or rectangles. Dip one side of each piece into the syrup. Using a spoon, spread the calisson cream evenly over each piece of brioche. Place them on a baking sheet, scatter over the chopped almonds and dark nougat, sprinkle with the confectioners' (icing) sugar, and bake in the oven for 10 minutes.

**CHRISTOPHE FELDER**   *Pastry Chef, Strasbourg*

# BUCKWHEAT FINANCIERS WITH DARK NOUGAT

**Makes 8 financiers**
**Prep: 15 minutes**
**Cook: 25 minutes**

⅓ cup (2 ¾ oz./75 g) butter + extra for the molds

Scant ½ cup (1 ¾ oz./50 g) ground almonds

⅔ cup unsifted (3 oz./85 g) confectioners' (icing) sugar

Scant ¼ cup (1 oz./25 g) buckwheat flour

2 ¾ oz. (75 g) egg white (about 2 ½ medium whites)

2 teaspoons apricot purée

A little flour for the molds

5 oz. (150 g) chopped dark nougat

Preheat the oven to 360°F (180°C). In a saucepan, melt the butter until it turns pale and smells slightly of hazelnuts. Strain the melted butter through a fine sieve and leave it to cool slightly.

Sift together the ground almonds, confectioners' (icing) sugar and flour. Stir in the egg whites, then add the melted butter and apricot purée. Mix with a whisk.

Butter and flour rectangular molds (unnecessary if you are using silicone molds). Using a spoon, fill the molds three-quarters full with the dough (the financiers should be at least 1 inch/3 cm thick) and cook for 17 minutes in the oven.

Using a pastry brush, apply a little dough on the financiers and scatter some chopped dark nougat on top. Bake for a further 3 minutes.

Remove the financiers from the oven, unmold them immediately, and enjoy them while still warm.

**PATRICE GELBART**  *Chef, Youpi au théâtre !, Gennevilliers*

# SLOW-COOKED PORK BELLY
## WITH SPICY DARK NOUGAT CRUST AND CARAMELIZED CARROTS

**Serves 4**
**Prep: 20 minutes**
**Cook: 4 hours 30 minutes**

**For the pork belly:**

1 lb. 5 oz. (600 g) fresh
black pig pork belly
5 carrots
1 celery stalk
1 onion stuck with 2 cloves
¾ oz. (20 g) peeled fresh ginger
1 strip of lemon zest
Soy sauce
Knob of butter
Salt, freshly ground pepper

**For the sweet-and-sour
nougat crust:**

3 ½ oz. (100 g) dark nougat
1 small fresh red chile pepper
¾ oz. (20 g) peeled fresh ginger
Juice and zest of 2 limes
1 bunch of cilantro (coriander)

Preheat the oven to 245°F (120°C). Put the pork belly into a casserole dish and cover with water. Add 1 carrot, peeled and sliced, the celery stalk, onion, ginger, lemon zest, and a little soy sauce. Lightly salt (the broth should reduce) and bring to a boil. Cover the casserole dish, put it in the oven, and cook for 3 hours.

Peel the remaining 4 carrots and add them to the contents of the casserole. Continue cooking for a further 1 hour. Remove the casserole dish from the oven, transfer the pork belly and whole carrots to a plate and leave to cool. Strain the broth and reduce to a syrupy consistency. Taste it and correct the seasoning. Set aside.

Prepare the sweet-and-sour nougat crust. In the bowl of a food processor, crush the dark nougat with the chile pepper, ginger, lime juice and zest, and cilantro (coriander).

Just before serving, brown the meat for 15 minutes in the oven at 360°F (180°C). Remove it from the oven and apply the nougat mixture over the entire surface of the skin, like a crust. Put the meat back in the oven for 5 minutes.

In a skillet (frying pan), lightly caramelize the carrots in a little butter. Reheat the gravy, adding any remaining nougat mixture.
Serve the pork belly with its colorful crust with the caramelized carrots and gravy, accompanied with a spicy salad mix of baby mustard and arugula (rocket) leaves, if you wish.

**PATRICE GELBART**  *Chef, Youpi au théâtre !, Gennevilliers*

# CANDIED PEAR
## AND NOUGAT CRUMBLE

**Serves 6**
**Prep: 30 minutes**
**Cook: 50 minutes**

2 ¼ lb. (1 kg) organic pears
Some fruit for decoration
(e.g. plums, figs)
½ cup packed + 1 tablespoon
(4 ½ oz./125 g) brown sugar
+ extra for the fruit

**For the crumble topping:**
¾ cup (3 ½ oz./100 g)
buckwheat flour
¾ cup (3 ½ oz./100 g)
bread flour
¾ cup (6 ½ oz./180 g) butter,
at room temperature
⅔ cup (2 ¾ oz./75 g)
slivered (flaked) almonds
⅓ cup (1 ½ oz./40 g)
chopped walnuts
2 ¼ oz. (60 g) nougat,
cut into small pieces

Preheat the oven to 400°C (200°C). Peel the pears, cut them in half, and remove the core. Cut the other fruits in half and pit (remove stone) if necessary.

Bake the fruit in two different dishes: place the pears cut side down in a square or rectangular baking pan. They should be packed in tightly. Arrange the other fruits on a small baking sheet or in a small baking pan. Sprinkle the pears with a thin layer of brown sugar. Bake all the fruits in the oven for about 30 minutes, until soft. Leave to cool.

Prepare the crumble mixture. Using your fingertips, mix together the flours, brown sugar, butter, almonds, walnuts, and nougat until the mixture has the consistency of breadcrumbs. Spread this over the pears without pressing it down. Return to the oven for about 20 minutes.

Serve the crumble warm or cold, cut into squares, with the baked fruits.

**STÉPHANE JÉGO** *Chef, Chez l'Ami Jean, Paris*

# CALISSON
# RICE PUDDING

**Serves 6**
**Prep: 20 minutes**
**Cook: 1 hour**
**Rest: 12 hours**

4 ¼ cups (1 L) whole (full-fat) milk

1 cup (7 oz./200 g) round (pudding or risotto) rice

10 calissons

5 teaspoons superfine (caster) sugar

7 oz. (200 g) white nougat, cut into small cubes

1 cup (250 ml) very cold whipping cream

The day before you want to serve the rice pudding, pour the milk into a large saucepan, then add the rice and calissons. Slowly bring to a boil and cook for 1 hour over a very low heat, stirring occasionally. The calissons will melt slowly and flavor the mixture, while the rice will become meltingly soft. Add the sugar and half of the white nougat, leave to cool, then transfer the rice pudding to a lidded container. Seal and refrigerate for at least 12 hours.

The next day, beat the whipping cream until firm, then gradually fold it into the rice pudding using a spatula. Transfer it to a serving dish and decorate with the remaining nougat.

**STÉPHANE JÉGO**   *Chef, Chez l'Ami Jean, Paris*

# CATALAN CREAM
# WITH CALISSON

**Serves 4**
**Prep: 15 minutes**
**Cook: 5 minutes**
**Chill: 6 hours**

1 cup (250 ml) whole
(full-fat) milk

1 cup (250 ml) whipping cream

1 vanilla bean

6 egg yolks

¼ cup (1 ¾ oz./50 g) superfine
(caster) sugar

12 calissons

In a saucepan, heat the milk with the whipping cream and split and scraped vanilla bean. Bring to a boil, then immediately remove from the heat. Cover the pan with plastic wrap (cling film) and let it steep.

In a bowl, beat the egg yolks and sugar until the mixture turns white. Gradually pour in the hot liquid, whisking continuously, then pour everything back into the pan and cook on a low heat, stirring with a spatula. Remove from the heat as soon as the mixture begins to thicken and stir for a few more minutes.

Place 3 calissons, cut in half, in the bottom of each ramekin. Pour the cream on top, cover the ramekins with plastic wrap (cling film) and refrigerate for 4–6 hours.

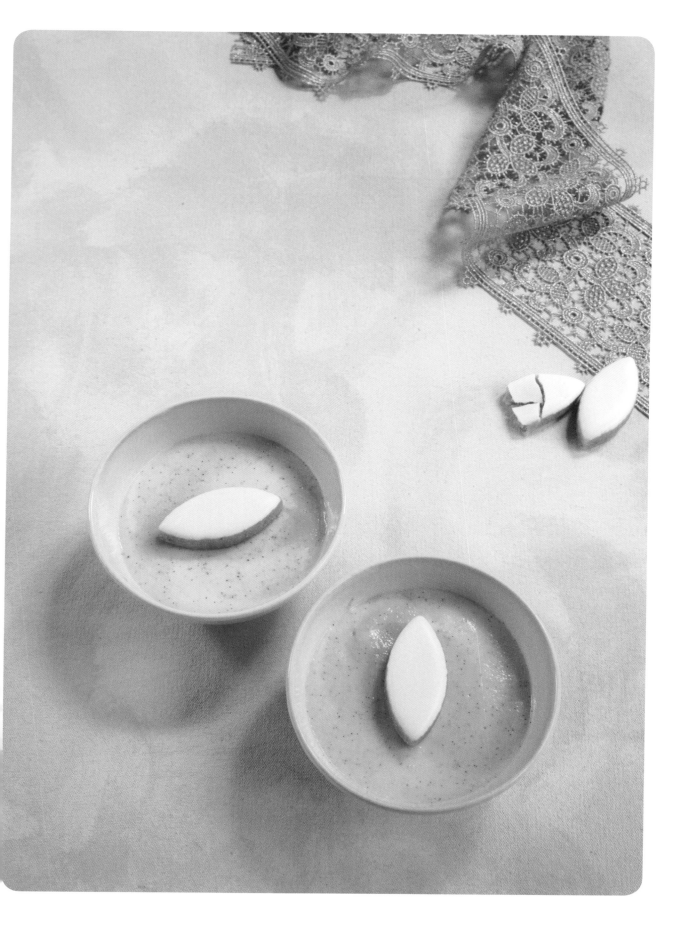

**GEORGIANA VIOU**     *Chef, Tindjan, Marseille*

**Serves 6**
**Prep: 20 minutes**
**Cook: 15 minutes**

6 ½ oz. (180 g) dark couverture chocolate, broken into pieces

½ cup (4 ¼ oz./120 g) butter + a little for the molds

3 eggs

Scant ⅔ cup (4 ¼ oz./120 g) superfine (caster) sugar

Generous ⅓ cup (1 ¾ oz./ 50 g) all-purpose (plain) flour

6 cubes of dark nougat

Preheat the oven to 360°F (180°C) on the fan-assisted setting. Melt the chocolate and butter in a bain-marie. In a bowl, beat the eggs and sugar until the mixture turns white. Stir in the flour, then the melted chocolate. Mix again until smooth.

Using a pastry brush, butter the cups of a muffin pan. Fill them two-thirds full with the mixture and place a cube of dark nougat in the middle of each one. Bake in the oven for 8–9 minutes.

Remove the fondants from the oven and leave to cool for 1 minute before unmolding and transferring to individual dishes.
Just before serving, make an incision in each fondant to reveal its melting nougat center.

# CHOCOLATE
# AND
# DARK NOUGAT
# FONDANT

**GEORGIANA VIOU**    *Chef, Tindjan, Marseille*

# NOUGAT
# GLACÉ

**Serves 4**
**Prep: 35 minutes**
**Cook: 5 minutes**
**Freeze: 4 hours**

3 ½ oz. (100 g) egg white
(about 3 medium whites)

⅓ cup (3 ½ oz./100 g) honey

2 tablespoons superfine
(caster) sugar

1 ⅔ cups (400 ml) very cold
whipping cream

5 oz. (150 g) white nougat,
chopped

Place the egg whites in the bowl of a mixer and whisk them until firm. Meanwhile, in a saucepan, bring the honey and sugar to a boil with a little water. Remove from the heat and wait until no longer simmering, then drizzle the syrup over the beaten egg whites, with the mixer still running. Continue beating until the meringue has cooled completely.

Whisk the whipping cream until firm, then gently fold it into the meringue. Carefully stir in the white nougat.

Pour the mixture into ramekins or a cake mold and place in the freezer for at least 4 hours. Remove the nougat glacé from the freezer 20 minutes before serving it, with some red-berry coulis, for example.

# For
# the
# King's
## PLEASURE

he splendor of the marriage between nougat and a duck breast or a roasted camembert. Calisson charmingly working its way, with its winning smile, into classic desserts, giving them a new twist. Beautifully presented but easily achieved sweet and savory dishes for breakfast, lunch, afternoon tea, or a dinner fit for a king. These clever recipes, by consummate culinary creator Sophie Brissaud, come as a surprise, revealing the taste of Provence and that of an inventiveness that turns every day into a celebration. Calissons and nougats become the ingredients for new pleasures, food for the imagination that can be varied in a multitude of ways.

# Niçois Chard Pie
## WITH WHITE NOUGAT

**Serves 6**
**Prep: 30 minutes**
**Cook: 40 minutes**

1 bunch of chard
1 tablespoon calisson cream
2 tablespoons diced candied fruit (e.g. lemon, orange, melon, and/or apricot peel, angelica, etc.)
1 apple
2 ¼ oz. (60 g) soft white nougat
2 pure butter pie crusts (ready-rolled shortcrust pastry circles)
Parmesan, to grate
⅓ cup (1 ¾ oz./50 g) pine nuts
4 thin slices of Parma ham
Confectioners' (icing) sugar
Extra virgin olive oil
Salt

Separate the green leaves from the chard and wash and dry them thoroughly (save the stalks for another recipe). Sauté them in a hot pan with a little olive oil, stirring until well wilted. Leave to cool, then press them between your hands to remove as much moisture as possible. Chop using a knife. Add the calisson cream, candied fruit, and a drizzle of olive oil. Season to taste with salt.

Preheat the oven to 360°F (180°C). Peel and core the apple and cut into thin strips. Chop the nougat into small pieces.

Lay one of the two pie crusts (pastry circles) on a plate, grate a little Parmesan in the center and place half of the chard mixture on top, forming it into a circle. Sprinkle over half the pine nuts and add a little more grated Parmesan. Cover with 2 slices of the Parma ham and half of the apple strips. Add the chopped nougat, then the remainder of the apple. Cover with the remainder of the ham, chard, and pine nuts (always respecting the shape of the circle). Finish by grating a little Parmesan on top. Brush the edge of the pie crust (pastry circle) with a little water and cover with the remaining pie crust (pastry circle). Press well around the edges to seal the pie, then cut away any excess pie crust (pastry), leaving a margin of about an inch (a couple of centimeters).

Make a few cuts on the top of the pie, brush it with olive oil, and bake it in the oven for about 30 minutes, until the pie crust (pastry) is turning golden.

Remove the pie from the oven, brush it again with olive oil, and sprinkle it with confectioners' (icing) sugar. Return it to the oven and bake for a further 5 minutes.

### Inspiration

The *tourta de blea*, a traditional recipe from Nice, exists in sweet and savory versions. This one is a combination of the two, which remains historically authentic in that sweet chard pies containing ham were once common.

### Le Roy's choice

Nougat and calisson cream naturally find their place in this recipe, which is actually less sweet than you might imagine. The aptness of this combination is both heavenly and surprising.

# Duck Breast
## WITH DARK NOUGAT

**Serves 4**
**Prep: 10 minutes**
**Cook: 15–20 minutes**
**Rest: 10 minutes**

2 duck breast fillets
1 ½ oz. (40 g) dark nougat
1 tablespoon calisson cream
Salt and freshly ground black pepper

Preheat the oven to 400°C (200°C). Cut the skin of the duck breasts in a crisscross pattern (being careful not to cut right through the skin). Rub them with salt and pepper and place them on a baking sheet or in a roasting pan.

Chop the nougat with a knife, then crush it lightly with the flat of the blade and a mallet to give small irregular pieces.

Brush the duck breasts with the calisson cream, then sprinkle generously with the crushed nougat (the calisson cream will help it stick to the meat).

Roast the duck breasts in the oven for 25 minutes. Check the coloring and the fusion of the nougat: the duck fat should have partially melted and the skin should be turning brown. Reduce the oven temperature to 360°F (180°C) and roast for a further 5–10 minutes, depending on how well cooked you like your meat. Remove the duck breasts from the oven and let them rest for 10 minutes before slicing them.

**Le Roy's choice**

The slight bitterness of the caramel reduces the sweet sensation, harmonizing well with the duck. A simple and elegant recipe that can be served with fresh figs or cherries, celeriac purée, and a green salad.

**Serves: 2–4**
**Prep: 5 minutes**
**Cook: 10–15 minutes**

1 mature rinded cheese (e.g. camembert, munster, Coulommiers, carré de l'Est, Époisses de Bourgogne, Maroilles, etc.) in a wooden box

1 ½ oz. (40 g) dark or white nougat

1 apple or pear

Freshly ground pepper

Preheat the oven to 360°F (180°C). Remove the paper wrapping the cheese and put the cheese back in its box. Cut a thin slice off the top of the cheese.

Cut the nougat into thin sticks that you can stud the cheese with. You won't be able to cut dark nougat into regular-size pieces; just do your best.

Wash the apple (or pear) without peeling it and cut it, too, into sticks.

Stud the entire surface of the cheese with the nougat and fruit. Grind over some pepper. Roast the cheese in its box in the oven for 10–15 minutes, until melted and sizzling. Serve immediately with teaspoons and some crispy bread.

# BAKED NOUGAT
# cheese

**Inspiration**

The classic baked camembert with garlic or truffle.

**Le Roy's choice**

The delicious fusion of cheese and nougat, plus apple, which adds a touch of freshness. Choose your nougat according to how strong the cheese is: use dark nougat for strong cheese, white nougat with creamier ones.

# CALISSON
# Almond Milk

**Serves 6**
**Prep: 5 minutes**

4 ¼ cups (1 L) unsweetened almond milk, chilled

2–3 tablespoons calisson cream

1 tablespoon orange flower or rose water

A few pinches of chopped dark nougat

Pour the almond milk into a blender and add the calisson cream and orange flower or rose water. Blend for 1–2 minutes, until the mixture is smooth and frothy.

Pour into glasses, making sure you distribute the foam evenly, and sprinkle with the chopped nougat. Serve immediately.

### Inspiration

Almond milk is a traditional cool drink from Northwest Africa and the Middle East.

### Le Roy's choice

Making almond milk is a long and tedious task. Store-bought unsweetened almond milk is a good substitute. For the rose or orange flower water, choose a real distillation rather than a commercial extract-based product, which will never have seen a flower. It will be more expensive, but infinitely better.

# Floating Island
## WITH DARK NOUGAT AND CALISSON CUSTARD

**Serves 4**
**Prep: 35 minutes**
**Cook: 30–35 minutes**

**For the custard:**
4 eggs
Scant 1 cup (200 ml)
whipping cream
2 tablespoons calisson cream
Scant 1 cup (200 ml) whole
(full-fat) milk
2 tablespoons superfine
(caster) sugar

**For the meringue:**
Pinch of salt
A little butter for the mold
1 ¼ oz. (35 g) finely crushed
dark nougat
2 tablespoons superfine
(caster) sugar
1 cup unsifted (4 ½ oz./125 g)
confectioners' (icing) sugar
1 handful of finely chopped
candied fruit (e.g. citrus peel,
apricot, angelica)

Make the custard. Break the eggs and separate the whites from the yolks in two different bowls. Add a pinch of salt to the whites and set aside (they will be used to make the meringue).

In a saucepan, mix the whipping cream and calisson cream. Add the milk and bring to a simmer, stirring with a spatula until the calisson cream has completely melted. Remove from the heat and cover.

In a bowl, using an electric hand mixer, beat the egg yolks and sugar until the mixture turns white. Gradually add the hot liquid, while continuing to beat. Pour the mixture back into the pan and cook over a low–medium heat, stirring well with a spatula until the mixture thickens. Remove from the heat, pour into a cold container, stir with a spatula for a few moments, cover, and refrigerate.

Make the meringue. Preheat the oven to 360°F (180°C). Butter a straight-sided charlotte mold or other tall and straight-sided mold. Add half the crushed nougat and rotate the mold to coat the sides. Set aside.

Beat the reserved egg whites until they begin to form soft peaks, then add the sugar—which will prevent the egg whites "weeping" later—and continue to beat until the mixture forms firm peaks. Using a spatula, stir in the confectioners' (icing) sugar, then the remaining crushed nougat. Pour this meringue into the mold, press it down, and smooth the surface. Cover the mold with foil, pierce it, and place the mold in a bain-marie. Bake for 25–30 minutes. Remove from the oven and remove the foil: the meringue should be firm and well risen.

Unmold the meringue into a dish and pour the calisson custard around the edge. Refrigerate until ready to serve.

# LEMON–CALISSON
# Mantou

**Serves 4**
**Prep: 40 minutes**
**Rising: 1 1/4 hours –**
**2 1/4 hours**
**Cook: 7–9 minutes**

2 cups (8 ¾ oz./250 g)
all-purpose (plain) flour
2 tablespoons superfine
(caster) sugar
1 teaspoon active dry yeast
or ½ oz. (15 g) crumbled
fresh yeast
Scant 1 cup (200 ml) warm milk
1 tablespoon candied
lemon peel
2 ½ tablespoons lemon
marmalade or lemon curd
7 or 8 calissons
A little white or dark nougat

Place the flour and sugar in a mixing bowl. Mix the yeast in a little warm water. Let it sit for 5 minutes, then pour the yeast into the bowl. Add the warm milk and the finely chopped candied lemon peel, then mix. On a floured surface, knead the dough by folding and flattening it, but without stretching it. It should become firm and elastic. Once it is no longer sticking to your fingers, knead it for a further 10–15 minutes until it is smooth, silky, and even more elastic. Shape it into a ball, put it back in the bowl, and cover with a damp clean kitchen towel. Leave the dough to rise for 1–2 hours, until it has doubled in volume. Knead it for a few more moments to expel any air.

Warm the marmalade to liquefy it. Finely chop the calissons and the nougat. Using a rolling pin, roll out the dough to about ½ inch (1 cm) thick and, using a pastry brush, spread it with a thin layer of marmalade. Sprinkle with the chopped calissons and nougat. Roll up the dough into a tight roll, then cut it into 1–1 ½ inch (3–4 cm) long sections. Place them on the rack of a steamer (removed from the steamer) and let stand for 10 minutes.

Boil water in the steamer, arrange the rack with the mantou on top, cover, and cook for 7–9 minutes. Remove from the heat without opening the steamer and let stand for 5 minutes. This will prevent the mantou from shrinking while cooling. Serve them hot with tea.

**Inspiration**

*Mantou* are leavened steamed buns from North China.

**Le Roy's choice**

With lemon marmalade, calissons, and a little nougat,
these mantou become an exquisite treat. They should be eaten hot,
but you can give cold ones a new lease of life by frying them
in hot oil until they are crispy and golden.

1 cup (250 ml) sticky rice flour
½ cup + 1 tablespoon (130 ml) hot water
1 ¾ oz. (50 g) dark nougat
1 tablespoon calisson cream
1 teaspoon dried osmanthus flowers (or 1 tablespoon orange flower water)
Cane sugar

**Inspiration**

Tang yuan is a Chinese dessert: sticky rice dumplings are stuffed with black sesame cream, chopped peanuts, or red bean paste. They are quickly poached then served hot in ginger syrup, in their cooking water sweetened with osmanthus flowers, or in tea.

Pour the sticky rice flour into a mixing bowl, add the hot water, and mix with a spatula until you have a smooth paste. If it seems too sticky, add a little more rice flour. If it is too firm, add a little more water. Let the dough rest for 3 minutes, then form it into a ball.

Chop the dark nougat with a knife as finely as possible. Mix it with the calisson cream until evenly distributed. Divide this mixture into little hazelnut-sized balls and count them.

Divide the rice dough into several pieces and roll them into sausage shapes. Divide these into as many walnut-sized pieces as you have nougat balls. Roll one of these rice-dough pieces into a ball, then, in the palm of your hand, flatten it into a disk with your fingertips. Place a nougat ball in the middle and fold over the edges of the rice dough to completely enclose it. Make sure that the dough is at least ⅛ inch (4 mm) thick all around the nougat ball. Continue until all the nougat balls are covered with rice dough.

Fill a large saucepan with water, bring to a boil, and add the tang yuan. Simmer until they rise to the surface, then continue cooking for 3 minutes. Drain them with a slotted spoon and divide among four bowls.

Empty some of the water from the pan, leaving enough to make a syrup. Dissolve some cane sugar (you can vary the amount according to your taste), then add the osmanthus flowers. Pour this syrup over the tang yuan and serve with porcelain spoons.

# Tang yuan
## STUFFED WITH DARK NOUGAT

# Toasted Brioche
## WITH FRESH FRUIT AND CALISSON

**Serves 4 (Makes 8 toasts)**
**Prep: 15 minutes**
**Cook: 15 minutes**

8 slices pure butter brioche
Softened butter (enough to spread over both sides of the brioche slices)
2 tablespoons calisson cream
Seasonal fruit (we used figs, raspberries, and grapes)
A few calissons

Preheat the oven to 320°F (160°C). Cut the crusts from the brioche slices to give you regular squares. Place the slices on a baking sheet.

Melt the butter and brush it onto both sides of the brioche slices. Brown them in the oven for about 10 minutes, keeping an eye on them: they should turn golden brown but not burn.

Remove them from the oven and spread with calisson cream.

Peel and slice the fruits, if necessary, and arrange generously on the toast. Chop the calissons with a knife and scatter over the fruit. Serve immediately.

### Inspiration

The initial idea was for a club sandwich, but it would have been a shame not to have fruit in this layering of ingredients. In addition, it was difficult to ensure a good balance. The toast solution is prettier, more delicious, easier to eat, and fruitier.

### Le Roy's choice

Calisson cream gives character to the simplest ingredients while elegantly enhancing them.

# Milk, Rose,
## AND CALISSON PASTILLA

**Serves 4**
**Prep: 20 minutes**
**Rest: 1 hour**
**Cook: 15–20 minutes**

1 ¼ cups (300 ml) whole
(full-fat) milk
2 teaspoons cornstarch
(cornflour)
2 tablespoons calisson cream
2 tablespoons rose water
¾ cup (3 ½ oz./100 g) whole
shelled almonds
12 calissons
½ cup (4 ¼ oz./120 g) butter
5 rectangular sheets of filo
dough (pastry)
A few dried rose buds

Mix a scant ¼ cup (50 ml) of milk with the cornstarch (cornflour). In a small saucepan, mix the remainder of the milk and the calisson cream. Heat gently, stirring with a spatula, until the calisson cream has dissolved. Bring to a boil, add a little hot milk to the cornstarch (cornflour) mixture, pour everything back into the pan, and leave to thicken over a low heat without stirring. Remove from the heat and add the rose water. Pour the creamy mixture into a bowl, cover with plastic wrap (cling film) and refrigerate for 1 hour.

Preheat the oven to 320°F (160°C). Spread the almonds out on a baking sheet, brown them in the oven for 5–7 minutes, then finely chop them with a knife. Chop the calissons.

Melt the butter. Butter two baking sheets and carefully lay the filo sheets on them. Butter them all over, then cut them into squares of equal size (allow about 12 squares per sheet). Brown the filo sheets in the oven for about 10 minutes, keeping an eye on them: they should turn golden brown but not burn.

Just before serving, assemble the milk pastillas: place a filo square on a plate and spread a little cooled cream on it. Add a few almond pieces, a few pieces of calisson and a pinch of crumbled rose buds. Cover with another filo square, then start again, making as many layers as possible.

Repeat for each plate and serve immediately.

**Inspiration**

Pastilla with milk is a light and crispy Moroccan dessert.

**Le Roy's choice**

The milky cream that accompanies the original version is even better when flavored with calisson cream. Because the dessert is assembled just before serving, the calissons' royal icing retains all its crispness, reflecting that of the almonds.

**Serves 4**
**Prep: 30 minutes**
**Cook: 30 minutes**
**Rest: 30 minutes**

10 ½ oz. (300 g) ripe seasonal
fruit (e.g. apples, pears,
peaches, nectarines, plums)
Pinch of salt
12 calissons
1 ¾ oz. (50 g) white nougat
1 tablespoon candied
lemon peel
Scant ½ cup (3 ½ oz./100 g)
butter, melted
5 rectangular sheets of filo,
brik or yufka dough (pastry)
Sugar, for sprinkling
Grated zest of ½ lemon

**Inspiration**

A legendary dessert,
the famous strudel of
the Austro-Hungarian
Empire, known as *rétes*
in Hungary.

**Le Roy's choice**

Contrary to what you
might think, strudel is not
difficult to make. Only the
preparation of the dough by
hand requires skill, but using
a dough in thin sheets such
as filo, brik, or yufka, also
gives good results. Seasonal
fruits add freshness to this
traditional pastry. Serve it
with whipped cream.

Preheat the oven to 360°F (180°C). Peel, core and pit (stone)
the fruit as necessary, depending on the fruit you have chosen.
Cut into small cubes and sprinkle with a little salt. Roughly chop
the calissons. Finely chop the nougat and the candied lemon peel.

Using a pastry brush, butter a baking sheet. Add a sheet of filo
and brush it all over with melted butter, being careful not to tear
it. Sprinkle it with a very thin layer of sugar. Cover with another
filo sheet and repeat until all the sheets are buttery and sweet.

Mix together the fruit, calissons, nougat, and grated lemon zest.
Lay the mixture in a sausage shape along the entire length of the
dough, about an inch (a few centimeters) from the lower edge.

Taking hold of this lower edge of the dough, roll the strudel from
the bottom to the top. As you do so, butter the surface of the
uncovered dough with a brush. You should finish with an even,
fairly tight roll. Generously butter the surface and sprinkle it very
lightly with sugar.

Bake for 30 minutes, until the strudel is golden brown. Remove it
from the oven, brush it with butter again, and leave it to cool for
30 minutes. Slice and serve it warm.

# NOUGAT-CALISSON
# Strudel

# Fruit Tart
## WITH CALISSON CREAM

**Serves 6**
**Prep: 30 minutes**
**Rest: 1 hour**
**Cook: 30 minutes**

**For the pie crust
(pastry base):**
2 tablespoons vegetable oil
2 tablespoons whole
(full-fat) milk
1 tablespoon sugar
Pinch of salt
Scant ½ cup (3 ½ oz./100 g)
butter, softened
1 egg yolk
About 1 ⅔ cups (7 oz./200 g)
flour (the quantity is judged
by the texture)

**For the filling:**
Seasonal fruits (e.g. apples,
pears, peaches, plums,
apricots)
2 tablespoons calisson cream
4 tablespoons ground almonds
1 egg
Scant ½ cup (100 ml)
whipping cream
12 whole shelled almonds
1 tablespoon brown sugar
1 spray bottle containing water

Make the pie crust (pastry). In a mixing bowl, whisk the oil, milk, sugar, and salt until the sugar has dissolved. Add the butter, whisking vigorously so that it absorbs the other ingredients and becomes creamy. Add the egg yolk, then gradually add the flour, while continuing to mix: the dough, which you need to shape into a ball, should be fairly soft. Wrap it in plastic wrap (cling film) and refrigerate for 1 hour.

Preheat the oven to 360°F (180°C). Remove the dough from the fridge and place it in the center of a pie plate (tart tin). Flatten it and, using your fingers, spread it out to the edge of the plate (tin) and up to the rim, making sure that the dough is of even thickness.

Make the filling. Peel, core, and pit (stone) the fruit as necessary, depending on the fruit you have chosen, then cut into thin slices. In a mixing bowl, using a fork, beat the calisson cream with the ground almonds, then add the egg and the whipping cream. Pour this mixture over the pie shell (pastry case), then quickly arrange the fruit on top and scatter over the whole almonds. Sprinkle with the brown sugar and spray with a little water.

Bake the pie in the oven for about 30 minutes, keeping an eye on it: lower the temperature if the almonds are getting too brown. Enjoy this tart warm or cold.

**Le Roy's choice**

Calisson cream gives an extra flavor to this simple tart. The pie crust (pastry base), which is surprisingly crumbly and sweet, is a recipe attributed to one Marie Laval, cook to a princely house of the Belle Époque. Spraying the pie crust (pastry base) with water accentuates the crispness of the sugar and almonds.

**Serves 4**
**Prep: 15 minutes**
**Cook: 20 minutes**

4 peaches
12 calissons
3 ½ oz. (100 g) dark or white nougat, finely chopped
Extra virgin olive oil or butter

Preheat the oven to 350°C (170°C). Cut the peaches in half and remove the pit (stone). Cut a small horizontal slice from the curved part of each peach half to make them very stable. Slightly hollow out the peach where the pit (stone) was to enlarge the cavity. Arrange the peaches, cut side up, on a baking sheet or in a roasting pan.

Chop the calissons with a knife and form the mixture into a compact ball. Divide this into eight balls and place one into each peach half. Scatter over the chopped nougat. Add a drizzle of olive oil or a small knob of butter to each calisson ball.

Bake for about 20 minutes in the oven, keeping an eye on them: the nougat should melt slightly and the peaches should be soft.

This dessert is best enjoyed warm.

# CALISSON-STUFFED
# Peaches

### Inspiration

A classic Italian dessert: peaches stuffed with amaretti.

### Le Roy's choice

It is easy to see how calissons can replace amaretti in this recipe. Everything is compatible: texture and flavors. A little dark or white nougat will add the finishing touch to this dessert. Dark nougat is less sweet and contains more almonds, while white nougat will add a soft and honeyed nuance.

# Chestnut and Dark Nougat Ice Cream

## ALMOND MILK AND WHITE NOUGAT ICE CREAM

**Serves 6**
**Prep: 25 minutes per ice cream**
**Rest: 4 hours**
**Strictly adhere to the setting time in an ice cream maker or freezer.**

**For the Chestnut and Dark Nougat Ice Cream:**
Scant 1 cup (200 ml) milk
Scant 1 cup (200 ml) whipping cream
4 egg yolks
5 teaspoons superfine (caster) sugar
8 ¾ oz. (250 g) crème de marrons (sweetened chestnut purée)
3 tablespoons marrons glacés (candied chestnuts)
3 tablespoons dark nougat

**For the Almond Milk and White Nougat Ice Cream:**
2 cups (500 ml) unsweetened almond milk
3 ½ oz. (100 g) plain marzipan
1 tablespoon calisson cream
4 egg yolks
¼ cup (1 ¾ oz./50 g) superfine (caster) sugar
3 ½ oz. (100 g) white nougat

Make the chestnut ice cream. In a saucepan, boil the milk and the whipping cream. In a mixing bowl, whisk the egg yolks with the sugar until they turn white. Pour the hot liquid over this mixture, while continuing to whisk, then pour everything back into the pan. Cook over a low–medium heat until the cream thickens. Using a spatula, gently fold in the crème de marrons until it has completely dissolved. Cover with plastic wrap (cling film) and refrigerate for at least 4 hours.

Chop the marrons glacés and finely crush the dark nougat, then add them to the mixture and transfer it to an ice cream maker.

Make the almond milk ice cream. In a saucepan, gently heat the almond milk with the marzipan, cut into small pieces, and the calisson cream. Mix until the marzipan has completely dissolved, bring to a simmer, and remove from the heat. In a mixing bowl, whisk the egg yolks with the sugar until they turn white. Pour the hot liquid over this mixture, while continuing to whisk, then pour everything back into the pan. Cook over a low–medium heat until the cream thickens. Stir back and forth with a spatula, cover with plastic wrap (cling film), and refrigerate for at least 4 hours.

Chop the white nougat, then add it to the mixture, and transfer it to an ice cream maker.

### Inspiration

Classic ice creams enhanced with crunchy nougat.

### Le Roy's choice

These recipes are equally delicious served separately or together.

**Makes about 20 cookies**
**Prep: 35 minutes**
**Cook: 15–17 minutes**

Scant ½ cup (3 ½ oz./100 g)
butter, softened
2 tablespoons confectioners'
(icing) sugar
2 egg yolks
1 ¼ cups (5 oz./150 g)
all-purpose (plain) flour
10 calissons
3 ½ oz. (100 g) white nougat

In a mixing bowl, beat the butter and confectioners' (icing) sugar using an electric whisk. Add an egg yolk and continue beating until light and creamy. Fold in the flour using a spatula. If the dough seems too firm, add a few drops of cold water.

Preheat the oven to 360°F (180°C). Chop the calissons and nougat and mix together. Form into a ball, then divide into ¾ inch (2 cm) diameter balls. Divide the dough into an equal number of balls.

Roll a dough ball in your hand, then flatten it in your palm and place a ball of the filling in the middle. Fold the dough around the filling to enclose it completely. Roll the ball into a slightly oval shape and place it on a baking sheet lined with parchment paper.

When all the cookies are on the baking sheet, make small incisions with the tip of a pair of scissors over the entire surface, always in the same direction, to give the appearance of a hedgehog's spines.
This is a delicate operation because you need to avoid cutting through to the filling.

Beat the remaining egg yolk with a few drops of water and lightly brush the cookies with it. Bake in the oven for 15–17 minutes, until golden brown. Leave to cool before serving.

# WHITE NOUGAT HEDGEHOG Cookies

### Inspiration

These little cakes come from Malaysia.
In their original version, they are filled with durian jelly.

### Le Roy's choice

Here, durian jelly is replaced with a nougat
and calisson filling.

# Torta Caprese
## WITH DARK NOUGAT

**Serves 6**
**Prep: 30 minutes**
**Cook: 1 hour**

3 ½ oz. (100 g) dark nougat
4 eggs
5 oz. (150 g) dark chocolate
⅔ cup (5 oz./150 g) butter +
a little for the molds
⅓ cup (2 ¾ oz./80 g) superfine
(caster) sugar
Scant 1 cup (3 ½ oz./100 g)
ground almonds
Confectioners' (icing) sugar,
for sprinkling

Preheat the oven to 360°F (180°C). Butter a fairly deep springform pan (cake tin), then line it with parchment paper.

Chop the dark nougat into small pieces with a knife or in a food processor. Break the eggs and separate the whites from the yolks. Melt the chocolate in a bain-marie. Using an electric mixer, beat the butter and half the superfine (caster) sugar, then add the melted chocolate. Add the ground almonds and chopped dark nougat and continue to mix.

Beat the egg whites until stiff with the remainder of the superfine (caster) sugar.

Using a spatula, and a circular motion from bottom to top, gently fold the beaten egg whites into the batter.

Pour the mixture into the cake pan (tin) and bake in the oven for 1 hour. Leave to cool completely before removing from the mold. Sprinkle the cake with confectioners' (icing) sugar before serving.

**Inspiration**

Torta caprese is a chocolate and crunchy almond cake from the island of Capri.

**Le Roy's choice**

The dark nougat adds an irresistible toasted and caramelized touch.

# LIST OF RECIPES

# MAJESTIC PROVENÇAL TREATS 98

# FOR THE KING'S PLEASURE 122

## — USEFUL ADDRESSES

**Église Saint-Jean-de-Malte**
(13th-century Gothic church with stained glass and paintings dating
from the 18th century)
24, rue d'Italie,
13100 Aix-en-Provence

**Musée du Calisson and Fabrique du Roy René**
5380, route d'Avignon,
13089 Aix-en-Provence

Find a list of Le Roy René stores at calisson.com

# — ACKNOWLEDGMENTS

Laure Pierrisnard, General Manager, and Olivier Baussan heartily
thank Pierre Reboul for his creative energy, as well as Chefs
Laila Aouba, Christophe Felder, Patrice Gelbart, Stéphane Jégo,
and Georgiana Viou for their kind participation in creating recipes
using the firm's iconic products: calissons d'Aix and white and
dark nougat from Provence.

A sincere thank you to memory-keepers Anne and Maurice Farine,
to our agricultural partners, especially André Pinatel and Jean-Pierre
Jaubert, to the Union des Fabricants du Calisson d'Aix, to the
Compagnons du Calisson, to the Association de la Bénédiction
des Calissons and its president Richard Flopin, to the Confiseurs d'Apt,
and to Félibrige in Aix-en-Provence.

Thanks, too, to Marie-Catherine de La Roche, Marie-Pierre Morel,
and Sophie Brissaud for beautifully highlighting our Provençal heritage,
to Camille Moirenc, François-Xavier Emery, and Fabien Quinard for
their photographs, and to Éditions de La Martinière.

Finally, a big thank you to the whole team at Le Roy René,
who proudly perpetuate the firm's *savoir-faire*.

Graphic design, production and
Illustrations for chapter openers: **Laurence Maillet**

Publishing: **Virginie Mahieux** and **Pauline Dubuisson**

Translation: **Anne McDowall**
English proofreading: **Nicole Foster**

Illustration page 84 : **Bernadette Baussan**

Recipes (pages 126-154) and recipe rewriting (pages 102-120): Sophie Brissaud

Abrams books are available at special discounts when purchased
in quantity for premiums and promotions as well as fundraising or
educational use. Special editions can also be created to specification.
For details, contact specialsales@abramsbooks.com or the address below.

Photoengraving: Quadrilaser
Printed and bound in February 2020 by Printer Portuguesa
ISBN: 978-1-4197-5074-8
Legal Déposit: March 2020
10 9 8 7 6 5 4 3 2 1
Printed in Portugal

195 Broadway
New York, NY 10007
abramsbooks.com